100 WAYS TO GAIN MORE SUCCESS

Through Promotion, Using Videos, and Building Your Business

Gini Graham Scott

Author of 200+ Books, including:
Increase Your Impact and Influence
Success Secrets in Everyday Life
Books for All Reasons

100 WAYS TO GAIN MORE SUCCESS

Copyright © 2019 by Gini Graham Scott

All rights reserved. No part of this book may be used or reproduced by any means, graphic, electronic, or mechanical, including photocopying, recording, taping or by any information storage retrieval system without the written permission of the author except in the case of brief quotations embodied in critical articles and reviews.

TABLE OF CONTENTS

INTRODUCTION 5
PART I: PROMOTING YOUR BOOKS, PRODUCTS, OR SERVICES 7
CHAPTER 1: 10 WAYS TO INCREASE YOUR CIRCLE OF INFLUENCE 9
CHAPTER 2: 10 WAYS TO PROMOTE YOUR BOOK, PRODUCT, OR SERVICE 33
CHAPTER 3: 10 WAYS TO USE SPEAKING TO GET CLIENTS AND MAKE SALES 57
PART II: USING VIDEOS SUCCESSFULLY 83
CHAPTER 4: 10 KEYS FOR CREATING A SUCCESSFUL VIDEO CAMPAIGN 85
CHAPTER 5: 10 WAYS TO CREATE AND USE A PROMOTIONAL VIDEO 109
CHAPTER 6: 10 WAYS TO PRODUCE A PROMOTIONAL OR INFORMATIONAL VIDEO 133
PART III: OTHER WAYS TO BUILD YOUR BUSINESS 157
CHAPTER 7: 10 WAYS TO ANALYZE YOUR OWN STRENGTHS, WEAKNESSES, OPPORTUNITIES, AND THREATS 159
CHAPTER 8: 10 WAYS TO GET INSPIRED WHEN YOU ARE FEELING STUCK 181
CHAPTER 9: THE 10 BIGGEST MISTAKES WRITERS MAKE IN PUBLISHING THEIR FIRST BOOK 203
CHAPTER 10: 10 WAYS TO FIND AND WORK WITH A VIRTUAL ASSISTANT 225
ABOUT THE AUTHOR 249

INTRODUCTION

100 Ways to Gain More Success is a combination of 10 short books that each features 10 ways to build your business through promotion, using videos, or otherwise expanding your influence.

These books are based on articles that originally appeared on Medium, and some were turned into PowerPoint presentations and videos.

The book is designed so you can write down your thoughts about how to implement each tip. In some cases, you might make a spreadsheet to keep track of what you do and the results to decide what methods work best for you.

The book is divided into three sections: Promoting Your Books, Products, or Services; Using Videos Successfully, and Other Ways to Build Your Business.

You can use these chapters in any order and choose those chapters that work best for you.

Now here are some tips on what to do.

PART I: PROMOTING YOUR BOOKS, PRODUCTS, OR SERVICES

CHAPTER 1: 10 WAYS TO INCREASE YOUR CIRCLE OF INFLUENCE

Your Circle of Influence plays a big role in your success, whether you are promoting books, workshops, products, or services. You might think of this Circle as the community around you, rather than the much larger audience that makes up your target market. Your target market can be a starting point, and you can pitch ads, publicity, and social media posts to them. But they don't become part of your Circle of Influence until they start to engage with you on a regular basis. Likewise, members of your family, friends, and business associates can become part of your Circle, but you have to proactively keep them involved in what you are doing so they become your supporters.

In other words, you want to create a Circle of Influence, which is variously referred to as your "raving fans," "tribe," or "connected community." Today, this Circle can be made up of both face-to-face contacts or virtual ones cultivated through repeated ongoing connections.

So how do you increase and motivate your Circle of Influence to support your latest projects, such as by talking about and buying your products, attending your programs, or using your services. Here are 10 ways to create and energize your Circle.

Use the blank page before each tip to write down your thoughts about how to apply that to increase your circle of weakness.

1) Join online social media groups, such as on Facebook or LinkedIn, which are reaching your target audience. But don't just start pitching whatever you are doing. Instead, take some time to introduce yourself and comment on the ongoing conversations. Then, after posting for a week or several weeks, depending on how often you make these postings, you can begin talking about what you are doing, share links to your website, or otherwise let group members know about your products or services. Then, if people respond favorably, remain in the group; if not, find other groups to join.

2) Consider participating in the trade associations or business groups that reach your target audience. For example, join or attend mixers of the local chambers of commerce in your area, and some might have business partner or links groups you can join. You might also find a variety of business referral and networking groups in your area. Typically, they have one person from each industry, and you might find the group members a good source of referrals. Another possibility is speaking at local chapter meetings or going to the annual conferences or business fairs of these groups. Consider being an exhibitor at these meetings, too. Once you find compatible groups with a good fit for your business, plan to continue going to the activities of the group, since a single meeting or mixer might not be enough to really connect with that community.

3) Look for opportunities to contribute to the blogs or magazines of the organizations that cater to your target audience. Commonly, you can write a single article and use it for multiple groups, since each group has its own audience, in contrast to writing an exclusive article for a publication with a national circulation.

4) Get in touch with the leaders of groups or with social media influencers in your field and offer them samples of your books, products, or online programs. If they like them, they may be likely to talk them up, resulting in multiple sales.

5) Create a blog or podcast in which you offer tips or information related to your book, product, or service, and that can lead people to want to know more by buying from you. What kind of content should you offer? A good start is to think of the problems you might solve for people in your niche, such as helping people fix up their homes, relationships, finances, or any other topic.

Another possibility is to entertain people in your Circle of Influence, such as recounting amusing experiences or observations, like the crazy things your dog or cat did today. Then, too, consider inviting guests to contribute articles to your blog or be interviewed on your podcast.

6) Start a video channel, where you feature regular talks to your audience, or perhaps you might turn PowerPoint presentations into videos. You can easily keep these presentations informal. Just set up a tripod with your phone or VSL camera and start talking; then save the file and upload it. If you want to edit your video, there are simple editing tools, such as Camtasia, where you can easily snip out sections of the video you don't like.

7) Post your videos on the social media. And keep them short — about 1-3 minutes, where you offer a few tips, do a demonstration, tell a story, or otherwise offer information or entertainment. At the end of the video or in the post below it, you can offer links to your website or landing page with more information about your products, services, and programs. As you keep doing this, a growing community of viewers will become regulars. And many will be receptive to clicking on the links in your post to learn more.

8) Develop an email list of people you meeting personally or through online activities, so you can send them regular emails or newsletters. When you meet people personally, such as at business networking events or trade shows, you can collect business cards and obtain the emails from them. If people don't have cards, you can invite them to write down their name and email on the back of one of your cards.

To get information online, one technique is to create a sales funnel sequence where you offer a free gift, such as a PDF with a few tips or a short informational webinar, and to get it, the person has to provide an email. Then, you set up an automated system to send the gift to their email and add that email to an autoresponder which will send out an email or newsletter with future offerings to them. And to get people to the start of the sequence, you use an ad or other promotion to get them to go to a landing page or page on your website. That's where you provide enticing information about the free gift, so they will want to give you their email to get it.

However, once you have an email list, use it sparingly — perhaps only send out mailings once every few weeks or each month, since too many emails can become a turn-off and even be labeled as spam.

9) Monitor the various activities you are using to build your Circle of Influence in order to assess which ones are working the best for you. A good way to do this is to create a spread sheet where you list the organizations and social media groups you have joined, the publications you have contacted, the blog posts you have created, and so on. Then, create a series of columns where you indicate what you have done, when, and the results, such as how many books or products you have sold, how many people have signed up for your workshops, and the like. After that, assess what groups and activities are most effective for you and continue to participate in them and cut back on or stop participating in the other groups and activities that are less effective.

10) Consider doing joint promotions with others with related books, products, or services in your target market, so you can engage in promotional activities together to reduce the cost and effort of whatever you are doing. For example, you can create a newsletter with a contribution from each of you; you can let organizations know you are available to do a panel together or speak individually; you can sign up to share a table at a trade show. You can also do a collective mailing to all of your email lists.

You can think of still other ways to expand your Circle of Influence. Whatever you do, keep track of the different things you are doing and the results to see what works best and keep doing that.

CHAPTER 2: 10 WAYS TO PROMOTE YOUR BOOK, PRODUCT, OR SERVICE

For a successful promotion of any book, product, or service, you need to use multiple channels directed at your target audience. This helps to make you more memorable and reinforces your visibility, credibility, authority, identity, and brand image. Whatever channel you choose, repetition helps to make your more memorable at a time when people are getting hundreds of messages a day from multiple sources. When people hear about your company, book, product, or service from different sources, this helps you stand out from the crowd.

Following are ideas for this promotion. Choose among them or try them all to see what works best. Then, track the responses you get from different approaches and continue to use those that work best for this or additional books, products, or services. This way, you will get even more attention when you launch additional projects.

As you read each tip, write down your thoughts about what to do for your promotion. Perhaps make a spreadsheet to keep track of what you do and the results. This will help you decide what methods work best for your promotions.

Now here are some tips on what to do.

1) Offer a free sample, such as a few chapters of your book, a trial membership for 7 to 30 days, an introductory webinar, or an entry into a lottery for a free product, in return for the person's email so you can deliver whatever you are offering and contact that person in the future with other offerings. Another possibility is doing a short webinar with valuable information to get the person to want more. Or use this approach to get people to hire you for a service by featuring samples of what you have done or offer tips the person can apply in their work or business. Then, promote your webinar with ads on the social media, such as on Facebook or Google, and see which ads perform the best with your selected target audiences. Again, get the person's email to send them further promotions. However, limit the number of future emails you send to every few weeks. Don't bombard your email contacts with too frequent emails or they may regard them as spam.

2) Create a monthly newsletter to send to your audience, and promote that in the social media where your audience is spending most of their time. If it's more of a business audience, use LinkedIn; for a more general audience, use Facebook; for a younger audience, try Instagram; and if you do a lot of your promotions on YouTube, send them to your YouTube channel.

3) Become a speaker and talk about your book, product, or service or offer tips based on it, such as how it can help solve a particular problem. Create a flyer or letter with the topics you talk about; then distribute or email them to organizations or companies who might like to hear from you. A good way to start is by contacting local groups and organizations, such as churches, community groups, schools, and business associations, to offer to speak to them. You can find lists of these groups through your local chamber of commerce or convention and visitors bureau; or put in a type of group along with the phrase "near me" or the name of your city in a Google search.

4) Hire a virtual assistant to help you with your promotional outreach, since it can be very time consuming to engage in all of these promotional activities. Virtual assistants can do things like manage your blog and social media posts, do research for you, or send out your press releases or letters to the media, podcasts, or radio shows.

You can find a VA by doing a search on Google for "virtual assistants near me" or your city. Some popular sources for finding them include Upwork, Fiverr, and services that connect virtual assistants with people who want to hire them, such as Zvirtual.com, Timeetc.com, Thumbtack.com, and uassistme.co. When you write or call, ask the VAs what they can do, and ask for examples of projects they have worked on. Rates are typically $20-40 an hour, or even less if you find a VA in other countries with lower costs, such as the Philippines, India, and Pakistan. Just be careful when you hire someone from another country that they are fluent in English and understand the business practices of your industry. And recognize the different time zones.

5) Team up with someone with a related book, product, or service to do joint promotions together. That can cut down your costs and effort. You might also share mailing lists or do a joint pitch or newsletter where you each send out these newsletters with information about both of you.

6) Start a regular blog on your website or on a blogging platform like Medium, where you can post tips related to your book, product, or service. Then, write a new blog every week or every few days to help you build up a following. You can even make money on your articles on Medium — not a lot when you get started, but posting there helps build your exposure, since the platform already has a built in audience.

7) Put on a local event, such as an open house or ribbon cutting ceremony, and promote it through your local chamber of commerce. If you are a member, they may feature it in their newsletter, or you can usually buy an ad in their publication. Also, look for community newsletters or magazines, which feature articles of interest to a local community. You might be able to get an article about your company, products, or services in the publication, and you can always advertise there.

8) Join a local business networking, referral, or mastermind group in your area. The networking and referral groups commonly only choose one person for each industry, and they can be a great source of customers and clients but referrals to their contacts. Most of these groups offer an opportunity to talk about whatever you do in a 7-15 minute presentation, and they encourage one-on-one or small group get-togethers so you can get together more personally.

The mastermind groups are typically groups of up to 10 to 12 members, and participants take turns presenting a problem or issue they are facing; then others provide feedback. You can ask for suggestions on how to promote your book, product, or service, and others may offer some great ideas for promotion. Often they can connect you with specific individuals or organizations who can help you.

You can also find mastermind groups held as Zoom meetings or through Facebook groups.

9) As you participate in any of these activities, contact your local media or community magazines to let them know what you are doing. Seek to develop a relationship with a local reporter or columnist, and keep them informed as you engage in new activities. After a while, you will become top of mind and they may be inspired to write a story about you.

10) Ask others who have done promotions what they have done that has been successful to get ideas for what to do yourself. Also, ask about what they have done which hasn't worked to help you decide what not to do. You can ask those you know in your community or business or in online groups.

In short, there are all kinds of ways to promote your book, product or service. And besides the suggestions on this list, you might think of still other promotional ideas. The key for a successful promotion is to select the approaches that are suitable to your particular audience and to use multiple strategies to reinforce your message. Then, look for those strategies which are most effective and double down on using those.

As you think of other ideas for promotion, write them down so you remember them. Later, you can consider what to do to implement different promotional ideas and monitor the results to choose to continue those that work best.

CHAPTER 3: 10 WAYS TO USE SPEAKING TO GET CLIENTS AND MAKE SALES

Speaking is one of the best ways to get clients and make sales of books, videos, or other materials, as well as get paid for your speaking. The advantage of speaking in various formats — from short talks to seminars and webinars — is it increases your visibility, credibility, and authority. Importantly, it will help you find clients and make sales of whatever you are selling — from books and video programs to products and services. And after you put on speaking programs for a while, organizations will pay you to speak, too.

Often people who hear you speak will want to hire you and buy any products or services you are selling. They may refer you to other organizations looking for speakers.

Initially, you may need to do talks, workshops, or seminars for free or for a small honorarium of about $50 to $100, but that's fine because these programs are a source of clients, sales, and referrals leading to future business. Over time, you may get paid more for your speaking, and at some point, this can turn into a major income stream. But first you generally need to build up your credentials as a speaker with a series of no pay or low pay talks and testimonials from attendees.

You can use your initial presentations to create a video or series of video clips from different programs to get additional speaking gigs. It's also important to create collateral materials to make a professional impression, such as having brochures and flyers with photos of you speaking, a list of your topics with descriptions, a bio, and any recommendations and endorsements you have gotten from others who have worked with you or heard you do presentations.

As you speak more, increase what you charge. Eventually, to position yourself as an expert on your topic, charge $5000-10,000, which is the going rate for an expert.

Regardless of whether you get paid or not for speaking, expect people to pay for consulting, coaching, or other services. Perhaps offer an introduction to what you do as an incentive, such as 20 to 30 minutes on the phone or in a one-on-one meeting to explore how you can help them. Or you might offer a free 30 to 60 minute strategy session to plan what they might do to build their business. But after that, expect to get paid.

Once you develop one or a few subjects to talk about, focus on speaking about them to different audiences, rather than trying to change your program to continually come up with something new.

As you read each tip, write down your thoughts about what to do to promote your speaking. Perhaps make a spreadsheet to keep track of what you do and the results. This will help you decide what methods work best.

Following are different ways you can use speaking to get clients and make sales.

1) Create a small format seminar for a small group of 4 to 12 people. You can meet in a conference room or around a table for coffee, lunch, or dinner. Then, use this gathering like a mastermind group, where you talk about how your expertise can help the participants and others offer their suggestions and advice. You can set up this small group meeting through local organizations, your mailing list, or create a Meetup group to offer such an event.

2) Contact organizations in your community which are looking for speakers and let them know you are available to speak about certain topics based on your area of expertise. You can contact these organizations by an email or phone call, and follow up with a flyer or document listing the topics you talk about. Indicate if you do seminars or workshops on these subjects, too. You can also target organizations in nearby communities. Some organizations to contact are local service clubs, such as the Rotary, Lions, or Kiwanis clubs in your community.

Other organizations to contact are local universities and colleges which have continuing education programs. You can offer a college course or extended study program on your topic. If you have a book on the topic, you can even require it as reading for the course, and as long as it's on topic, it's both fitting and ethical to do so. Many of your students may also want to learn more or hire you as a consultant.

3) If your topic might be of interest to corporations, such as programs on marketing, increasing productivity and profitability, team building, or improving relationships, you can pitch your paid talk or workshop to whoever handles guest speaking arrangements for the corporation.

You can get a list of companies through the local chamber of commerce or through a directory of companies in your area, such as the Book of Lists, published by the *San Francisco Business Times*. You can also find companies and contact information on LinkedIn. Another source of leads is Vistage, which has over 23,000 members from companies with $500,000 or more in annual sales revenue and chapters around the country.

In your pitch to the corporate market, charge $5000-10,000 as an expert. If you price your program too low, the officials who set up these programs might not take you seriously.

4) Organize a public seminar or workshop, charge admission, and promote this by yourself or with others. Generally, charge $10 to $25 for general admission to a 60-90 minute seminar. For follow-up in depth programs lasting several hours or longer, you can charge more.

Some good venues for holding seminars include a room in a library, at a college with an adult extension program, or a conference room in a bank, hotel, or country club. If your program would be of special interest to the employees or officers at a large corporation, choose a room near that company's offices and promote the program to the people there.

Another approach for these public programs is to use them as a fundraiser, where you share the proceeds with the organization or association that will promote it to its members and mailing list, as well as do other marketing and publicity for the program.

5) Be a keynote speaker, where you speak for about 30 to 45 minutes at a luncheon, dinner, or conference for an organization or association. In this case, make your program entertaining as well as informative, such as by including stories to illustrate the different points you are making.

Alternatively, offer to be a leader of a breakout session on your topic at a conference, which usually has about 15 to 50 people. Or offer to be on a panel or organize a panel, where you are the moderator and can usually speak as one of the panelist, too.

6) Pitch yourself to be a guest on a podcast. These are ideal because they typically stream, so people can listen whenever they want, such as when driving, going on a hike, or working out at the gym. By contrast, radio shows are commonly aired at one time, though some become archived and are much like podcasts, such as shows on BlogTalkRadio.com.

It's better to be a guest than have your own show, since the host already has a built in audience. You can certainly start your own podcast or radio show, but you have to build your audience, which can take much time and efforts.

Getting on TV shows can be fine, but you tend to be on for just a few minutes and once it's over, it's over. However, adding a TV show to your bio contributes to your credibility and authority.

7) Team up with others who are speaking on related areas, where you can pitch yourself as either individual speakers or part of a panel. This way you can market your programs together through joint mailings or flyers, or you can exchange email lists or promote each other in your emails.

8) Organize a retreat on your topic. You can do this yourself or combine forces with others. In this case, find a nice place to hold the event, such as in the countryside near you. You can rent a house for a couple of days through Airbnb, HomeAway, or other short-term home rental service and hire someone to cater or order food from a local restaurant. Then, you schedule a series of talks and workshops throughout the day.

Or for a more local or short-term program, such as for a day or half-day, you can find office or meeting space, which is rented by the hour or day through companies like Industrious, OfficeEvolution, Regis, and WeWork.

9) Set up a teleseminar or webinar, such as on Zoom or GotoMeeting. Introductory teleseminars and webinars are ideal for introducing you and your products or services by giving attendees some valuable information about your topic. hen, you offer a more in-depth program, such as a workshop, retreat, online course, or several hours of consulting at a special rate. For instance, you might offer a dramatically lower reduced rate for the next day or two for those participating in this introductory program to entice them to sign up for your offer now.

10) Still other possibilities:
- Record your talks and create audio recordings for sale, or combine them on a flash drive or DVD with your book and sell them together.
- Create short how-to videos of about 1 to 2 and at most 3 minutes, where you share some valuable tips on how to do something in your topic area. One good way to create these videos is to hire a professional videographer to come to one of your speaking engagements and record your talk. Then, you can cut that full video into very short how-to clips and post them on YouTube. Additionally, you can sell an edited video of your complete talk — or use the complete video as part of an online course made up of a series of videos. Still another way to do these videos is to set up a VSL camera or your phone on a tripod, sit in front of the camera, and talk. Or combine a short 15-20 second introduction of you talking with a PowerPoint turned into a video using text-to-voice technology to create a narrative for the video as it plays.
- Participate in a 50-50 event sponsored by a promoter, where you appear on stage if you have some kind of product, such as a book, video, or other package of information. You get to talk briefly about your topic and the products you have and split the proceeds with the promoter.

So there you have it — 10 different ways to use your speaking to get clients, sell any books or products, and eventually get money for your speaking. I've used many of these techniques or have heard them recommended by professional speakers.

Maybe you can come up with other ideas. Write them down as they come to you.

Now get started by turning whatever you are doing into topics you can talk about to get clients and sales.

PART II: USING VIDEOS SUCCESSFULLY

CHAPTER 4: 10 KEYS FOR CREATING A SUCCESSFUL VIDEO CAMPAIGN

Creating a short video is a powerful tool for increasing your credibility and getting people to pay attention to you. The stats on videos show why creating videos to promote yourself, your business, or your products and services is so important today. Social video results in 1200% more shares than both text and images combined, according to SmallBiz Trends. If you put a video on a landing page, that can increase the conversion rate for your sales by 80%, according to Hubspot.

Using videos is so powerful because a video done right increases your credibility. It helps to create rapport and connection with your audience. It makes you more likeable and helps people believe in you and trust you. And people like to do business with those they know, like and trust.

Now you can create short videos in minutes with a few clicks on your phone. There's no need for an expensive production, because people like the intimacy of seeing you up close and personal. Even the big stars create these informal videos, and now you can even hire many well-known personalities to give you a shout-out. Check out Cameo.com for details.

Here are some keys for having a successful video campaign. Use the blank page before each tip to write down your thoughts about how to apply that tip in your own video campaign.

1) Decide on your niche and target audience. Plan what you want to say and how to say it to reach that audience. Then, imagine that you are speaking to an individual in that audience, like you are having a conversation with that person when you create your video.

2) Pick one tip or benefit you can offer your target audience in each video. Keep it short, about 30 seconds to 2 minutes. Then, talk about how you can help with that one thing. In picking the tip or benefit to offer, pick a problem that you can help solve and offer a solution.

3) Try out different types of videos to determine which one or ones your audience likes best. Use alternative approaches for variety. The major types of videos are: a demonstration or tutorial; offering a few short tips about something; an interview with another person; sharing informal advice and insights.

4) Select a good setting for your video. You can select a single setting you use each time, such as your office, living room, or workroom. Or you can have varied backgrounds, such as if you travel a lot or do workshops in different locations.

5) Use a consistent format, which contributes to building your identity or brand, such as having the same background or logo behind you. Some other formatting tips are these. Use a tripod and horizontal format to better show and demonstrate things as you talk. Use a selfie-stick and a vertical format to be more conversational and informal. Perhaps begin each video with a signature introduction, such as holding up a poster or banner with your name, company, or tagline.

6) End each video with a call to action indicating what you want the audience to do. Some possibilities are:
- Give you their email to get a free gift or join your newsletter list.
- Buy your book or product.
- Sign up for your event, workshop, or webinar.
- Arrange a strategy session with you by phone or Zoom.
- Forward your video to a friend or business associate.
- Join you in the next day or two for more information.
- Go to your website for more free information (and provide their email to get it).
- Or more.

Whatever you are offering, ask viewers to click the link below the video to take the next step.

7) For an effective video, prepare what you want to say. Create an outline of your major talking points or write out a script, as you prefer. If necessary, create cards with large type and put them on an easel in front of you, so you can read from them, like with a teleprompter, but keep whatever you say conservational and real — not like you are reading.

8) Have a consistent look that fits your brand, so dress the part. Look professional and select strong and plain colors. Avoid patterns and logos. And don't wear anything wild and crazy, unless you want to create that the kind of character.

9) Include one or more soundbites, which are parts of your interview that are especially powerful and catchy. These one-liners will help to make your video more memorable, and viewers may quote you, and they'll be more likely to share your video.

10) Think of how to give value in each video, so people will want to watch. But be brief, so you focus on a particular point, which makes your message more memorable. Also, practice, practice, practice to get your presentation right, especially when you are starting out. After you do a series of videos, it will be faster and faster to make them, because they will become like a regular practice or habit. So it will be easier to create these videos more quickly, and you won't need to practice as much or at all.

CHAPTER 5: 10 WAYS TO CREATE AND USE A PROMOTIONAL VIDEO

Now that video has become so important in gaining attention and visibility, you want to do it effectively, while keeping your costs down. There are many things you can do yourself at low or no cost, unless you have the budget to bring in a professional videographer, who typically charges $75-125 an hour.

One important place to use videos is on your website or landing page to help visitors decide to hire or buy from you. As researchers have found, a video on your landing page can up your conversion rate from views to sales by 80% or more.

Another place to use videos is with your social media posts, blog posts, or articles on a platform like Medium. You'll increase the number of viewers, likes, visits to your profile, hires, sales, and more.

Video has this power to attract clients and customers because it increases your credibility, authority, and visibility. It builds your professional image. It also helps your audience feel closer to you because it makes you seem more likeable and accessible, which builds trust. And as they say again and again in business groups: people want to do business with people they know, like, and trust.

So how can use video most effectively to promote you and your business? Following are a series of tips on how to do that.

As you read each tip, write down your thoughts about what to do to. Perhaps make a spreadsheet to keep track of what you do and the results. This will help you decide what methods work best.

Now here are the tips on what to do.

1) Use a script as a guide so you know what you want to say and do so concisely and compactly. Then, rehearse, rehearse, rehearse, so you are fully prepared when you go on camera, unless you are an expert at winging it, which most people aren't. You don't have to memorize everything word for word. Just remember the main bullet points you want to make. Alternatively, use a teleprompter, where you write out everything or list bullet points. Then, rehearse a few times, so you can easily say what you have written. You don't want to sound like you are reading form a teleprompter.

In preparing your script, keep your video short and focused on the main points you want to make. Keep it to 30 seconds to 2 minutes, and up to 3 minutes max. The shorter your video the better to get your point across, because people have a short attention span today.

2) Decide on the type of video you plan to do. Some possibilities include a video with tips, an introduction to a short video made from a PowerPoint, or an interview with another person about your topic. Whatever your format, focus on a single subject of interest to your target audience. Include a call to action at the end, such as to go to your website, get a copy of something, watch a particular video, or go to a landing page for a free sample of something.

Whatever format you use, provide value to your target audience by solving a problem for them with your advice. Think about the challenges or difficulties they might face or the questions they might have about something. Then, you provide the solution by giving a series of tips, talking about the problem with another person, or doing a demonstration on how to make or do something.

3) Besides the shorter promotional 1-3 minute videos, consider doing longer tutorial videos for viewers who are more seriously interested in the subject. In these longer videos, you go into more detail in explaining or demonstrating something. Such videos commonly range from 5 to 15 minutes, and they are ideal as individual modules or classes if you are creating an online course or webinar.

4) Conclude your video with a call to action, which you can also include in a social media post when you use that to link to your video. For example, you might invite people to buy your book or product, sign up for your webinar, try your service, come to an introductory strategy session, or get a special package price on one of your programs.

5) You can create these videos in various ways, depending upon your equipment. If you are producing the videos yourself to keep down costs, you can use the camera on your computer or on your phone, or if you have a DSLR camera which can shoot videos, you can use that. When you use a camera, put it on a tripod, and unless you are only posting on Instagram, set it up horizontally, so it looks more like a professional video.

    Ideally, use natural lighting, which will give you a more natural look. If you use any lights, get bulbs that mimic natural lighting.

6) If possible, do the video in one take, so you don't have to edit it. However, you can do simple editing on a platform like Camtasia. Then, you can easily cut out beginnings, endings, or sections you don't want, and after you make a cut, you can push any separated sections together. This will result in a jump cut, which is fine for simple editing, though if you are more skilled in editing, you can add dissolves and fades where you make a cut.

7) Turn your video into a blog post by pulling out the audio and having it transcribed; then edit the transcription to create the blog post. Alternatively, turn a blog post into a video by talking about what you have written or by putting the copy into a PowerPoint presentation and turning that into a video. Then, if you want, you can introduce the PowerPoint video.

8) Use your phone to capture in-the-moment videos to add a personal touch and build rapport with your audience. You can either post these videos later livestream them on Facebook, Instagram Stories, or YouTube Live. Later, you can download and post them on your website or landing page. You can send links to your video via email, too.

9) However you create your video, post it or a link to it on all of the social media channels, including Facebook, Twitter, and LinkedIn. Create a YouTube channel so you can post it there. Then, you can link to that YouTube posting or embed it on your website or landing page, rather than posting the video directly. That way your website or landing page will load faster than if you upload a lot of large video files.

A single YouTube channel is fine if your videos are centered around a particular theme or topic. But if you have different topics for different audiences, create separate channels for these. For example, if one topic is resolving conflicts in organizations and another is helping individuals find career success, it might be better to create separate account for each one.

You can also include a link to your video in an email to your contacts and prospects, and that link will result in a much higher clickthrough and response rate.

10) Post your videos consistently on the social media or YouTube, so people come to follow you, because they like what you are doing. The video on your website can be a more permanent fixture, though you can update this from time to time as you engage in new activities and create new videos.

Besides posting your video individually on various platforms, you can use a program like HootSuite or Buffer to send out your social media posts with a video to multiple channels at the same time. You can send out each post immediately or schedule a series of posts for several days, weeks, or even several times a day. For example, I use HootSuite to send out a few posts with videos or images to 10 different social media channels a few times a week.

Now get started creating and promoting your own videos.

And you may have other ideas on what to do. If so, write them down on the preceding page.

CHAPTER 6: 10 WAYS TO PRODUCE A PROMOTIONAL OR INFORMATIONAL VIDEO

Once you plan to create a promotional or informational video, what's the best way to produce it, whether you are doing it yourself or using a professional videographer? Assuming you will be featured in the video, you want to come across as being very knowledgeable and confident, yet warm, friendly, and accessible. You also want to dress to fit your topic and choose clothing that photographs well. Here are some tips on how to look and sound your best.

As you read each tip, write down your thoughts about what to do to. Perhaps make a spreadsheet to keep track of what you do and the results. This will help you decide what methods work best.

1) Determine in advance what you want to talk about and stay focused on that topic, so each video features one idea. Prepare a script or bullet points to guide you, and rehearse at least a few times, so you have a polished presentation.

If it fits your topic, include stories, since those can illustrate the points you are making, and people really like and remember them. But keep your stories short, just a few sentences to feature the highlights of what happened. You don't want to go into long details, just enough to tell your story in 15 to 30 seconds.

If you are being interviewed by an interviewer, prepare a list of questions and answers in advance as a guide for the interviewer and yourself. Consider the interview like a conversation, so keep your responses short and to the point. Don't keep talking in response to a question like you are giving a speech. Rather, think of the conversation like a tennis match, where you keep sending the ball back and forth, as the interviewer sends you a ball to hit back.

2) Set up the camera with a horizontal screen, unless you only plan to post your video on Instagram, which features square images.

Also, set up the camera so it is eye level, so you can look directly at the camera and not up and down. Unless you are using the camera on your computer, use a tripod, so you don't have a moving camera that is distracting. Generally, selfie-sticks are not a good idea for promotional videos, since they jiggle around, though they are fine if you are traveling somewhere and want to invite to viewer to a more personal visit with you.

3) Look into the eye of the camera, not at your image on the screen, so you appear to be talking directly to the viewer. This helps them feel more of a connection with you.

If you are talking to an interviewer or an audience, focus on the interviewer or one person in the audience and look them in one eye. This way you stay focused on that one spot, which will help you concentrate on your topic rather than worrying about where to look.

4) Speak up to project your voice. Even though you might be alone with the camera, imagine that you are talking to a full audience and they are eagerly listening as you talk.

5) Remember to smile and be warm and friendly. If you tend to have a serious look, remind yourself to keep smiling, and even set up a trigger as a reminder, such as putting a small string on your finger or wearing bracelet or band on your wrist.

6) When making a series of points on a subject, use a breath between statements to pause for a second or two. This pause can give more emphasis to each point you are making.

7) Wear something that fits the topic you are talking about. If it's a serious business topic, wear a suit. If it's on how-to techniques to fix up your house or car, dress as you would to make the repairs. If it's a self-help topic, dress comfortably and casually, as if you are consulting with a client. The idea is to dress as a professional based on whatever work you do.

Also, pick a color scheme which photographs well on camera. Choose bold or plain colors. Avoid plaids, stripes, and patterns, since they look busy and detract from you. Select something with a strong enough fabric to hold a microphone if you will be wearing a clip-on mic.

Additionally, avoid anything that might jangle as you speak, such as heavy jewelry or necklaces, pins, or bracelets with dangling pieces. And don't wear a hat, because it can obscure part of your face, and it can look weird if you are doing an indoor shoot, unless this is your usual style.

8) Think about something that might be a soundbite, which media people and others might use to describe your video. This is a short phrase or statement that is especially catchy or impactful. You can sprinkle these soundbites through your talk or interview, and it will help your video stand out and get others to talk about it. An example might be a summary point you make after describing the benefits of your book, product, or service, such as "It's a mysterious family saga where people keep disappearing," or "You might call this a quick energy charger, because it will charge you up for anything you want to do."

9) Include a call to action in the end, and plan out what it will be and how you will state this. For example, a call to action might be something like: "Click the link below this video to find out more," and you point downward in the video so the viewer's eye will go down. Or say something like: "Go to my website to sign up now and get the big bonus for the first 25 to sign up." Then, your website link with the bonus offer flashes on the screen below you as you talk or immediately afterwards.

10) Practice several times before you record the video, and if possible, do it in one take, so you don't have to do any editing.

If you use a script, you can put it on a teleprompter or create and remember some bullet points to guide you in what to say. You can buy a teleprompter to attach to your camera, smartphone, or iPad for as little as $30, though most cost $200 to $400. Just put "teleprompter" and "near me" in Google Search to see a number of teleprompters for sale.

If you find creating these videos difficult, try signing up for media training. Look for a class on this to keep costs down, though you can work individually with a media coach. Preferably, look for a media training program in your area, though some media coaches can do these trainings online, such as on a Zoom platform where everyone can see everyone. In these trainings, you record yourself; then you, the media coach, and any classmates view it and comment on what was good and how you can improve.

Now start producing your own videos. And you may have other ideas on what to do.

PART III: OTHER WAYS TO BUILD YOUR BUSINESS

CHAPTER 7: 10 WAYS TO ANALYZE YOUR OWN STRENGTHS, WEAKNESSES, OPPORTUNITIES, AND THREATS

A SWOT analysis has long been used by organizations and corporations to make decisions about how to improve the organization and its products and services to increase sales and profits. But you can use it to improve yourself, your performance, and your work. Here are 10 tips on how to do this so you become a better you.

Use the blank page before each tip to write down your thoughts about how to apply that tip in analyzing your own strengths, weaknesses, opportunities, and threats.

1) In a SWOT analysis, you assess your Strengths, Weaknesses, Opportunities, and Threats and decide what to do about them. You want to build on your strengths, overcome key weaknesses, take advantage of opportunities, and confront or avoid any threats. To do so, first analyze your situation in each area. Then, consider what to do and prioritize what you want to work on in each area. Also decide whether to work on your strengths, weaknesses, opportunities, or threats first, and what to work on next, and next after that.

2) Besides doing a SWOT analysis on your own, you can do it with a partner or in a group, which can be especially helpful, because you get both support and insights from others. Then, this feedback from others along with your own ideas can help know what to do to in addressing each of these areas.

3) To keep track of your assessment for each area, create a chart to do this analysis. List each category, and next to it, set up two columns. In one column, record your thoughts about what to do, and in the next column, indicate what action you plan to take and when.

4) First think about your Strengths. These can be both personal qualities or strengths you gain from others in your personal life or work. Ask yourself: What do I do best? What do most like to do? How can I do more of what I do best or what I most like to do? Also ask: What are the strengths I gain from others I associate with or from my work? How can I further benefit from these relationships? If you are doing this analysis with others, ask for their suggestion on what to do.

Then, decide what you want to do and put a number and date next to each item on your to do list to indicate what you want to do first, second, and so on, and when you will do it.

5) Next think about your Weaknesses. These can be in yourself or in your relationships in your personal life or at work. Ask yourself: What are my biggest weaknesses? Why do I consider these weaknesses? How are they holding me back? What do I want to do to change and improve them? Is there anyone who can help me improve? If you are doing this analysis with others, ask for their suggestion on what to do.

Then, decide what you want to do and put a number and date next to each item on your to do list to indicate what you want to do first, second, and so on, and when you will do it.

6) Now think about your Opportunities. These are things that are outside you, such as opportunities for new relationships, jobs, or business possibilities. Ask yourself: What are the opportunities I have now in my personal life or work? Which opportunities are most valuable or important to me? What can I do now to take advantage of these opportunities? What can I do in the future to take advantage of them? Is there anyone who I can invite to take advantage of this opportunity with me? If you are doing this analysis with others, ask for their suggestion on what to do.

Then, decide what you want to do and put a number and date next to each item on your to do list to indicate what you want to do first, second, and so on, and when you will do it.

7) Finally, think about your Threats. These are generally things that are outside yourself that could harm you, such as a financial threat, threat from another person or threat of a job or business loss. But you could also face internal threats, such as a personal failing or lack of some quality, such as a lack of courage or self-confidence that is getting in the way of something you want. Whatever the threat, identify it and think of ways to overcome it. Ask yourself: What are my biggest external or internal threats? How are they affecting my life now? What is the risk of facing these threats in the future? What can I do to overcome the threat? Who can I call on to help me overcome the threat? If you are doing this analysis with others, ask for their suggestion on what to do.

Then, decide what you want to do and put a number and date next to each item on your to do list to indicate what you want to do first, second, and so on, and when you will do it.

8) Now decide on the order in which you want to work on your strengths, weaknesses, opportunities, or threats. Then, start taking the actions you have identified to take in that category.

9) Keep a record of what you do and the results. Note significant accomplishments and praise yourself for that achievement. Take some action to reward yourself, such as giving yourself a gold star, taking a day off to do something fun, or treating yourself to a visit to a spa. Perhaps tell others about what you have accomplished and enjoy their kudos.

10) Notice how your life has improved as a result of doing a SWOT analysis on yourself, and praise yourself even more for what you have done. Plan a special celebration to honor your progress, such as a get-away trip for a few days or a gala party with friends and associates to tell others how much you have changed because of the SWOT analysis. You might also suggest that doing this analysis can help others, too.

CHAPTER 8: 10 WAYS TO GET INSPIRED WHEN YOU ARE FEELING STUCK

Everyone experiences times when they feel stuck in coming up with ideas for writing or for doing anything. They feel unmotivated, stressed, or distracted by other things that are going on.

Here are some surefire ways to get your creative juices going and feel motivated again.

Use the blank page before each tip to write down your thoughts about how to apply that tip to get over feeling stuck.

1) Practice a technique called "mindfulness." When you are mindful, you pay attention to what is happening in the present moment without judgment. You calmly acknowledge and accept your feelings, thoughts, and bodily sensations. A good way to practice mindfulness is to find a time to do this for about 20 to 30 minutes, ideally in the morning to start the day. Go to a quiet place, get comfortable, and sit up straight but stay relaxed. Then, pay attention to what your arms and legs are doing, while you relax your whole body. You'll feel much better and ready to go after the process.

2) Use guided meditation, so you focus on a particular question or topic where you feel blocked or want some insight. Get relaxed as you would for a regular meditation session in a quiet place. Turn out the lights or use a cloth to cover your eyes. Then, ask your question or state the subject for which you want some insight. After that, let your intuition or unconscious mind take over. Don't try to think or direct your thoughts. To help you remember, take handwritten notes or record your ideas on a recording device as they come to you.

3) Engage in a routine exercise, where you can let your mind go and don't have to think about what you are doing. Find a place to exercise without others around. For example, run around your backyard, move or dance to relaxing music in a dark room at home, or lie on your back and move your legs back and forth. Then, ask yourself a question or state a topic you want to think about as in a guided meditation, and let the ideas come to you.

4) Have a conversation with your pet — or imagine a pet is sitting in front of you. Then, tell your pet what is bothering you and ask what you should do to stop your negative feelings. After that, ask your pet for ideas for what to do to fix whatever is wrong and listen to what your pet says.

5) Put a picture you view as relaxing or inspiring on the wall or on a stand in front of you. Then, gaze at the picture and let yourself flow into the picture. Let your rational mind go and see where the picture takes you. When you feel very relaxed and are wherever the picture has taken you, ask any question you want and see what ideas come to you.

6) Set aside 30 minutes to an hour or two to concentrate on writing or coming up with ideas for your project. Even if you feel restless, commit yourself to spending that time and be open to whatever comes to you. For example, sit at your computer or open your journal, and write whatever comes to you.

7) Keep a journal by your bed. Before you go to sleep, when you are in that very relaxed state before you fall asleep, tell yourself that you will dream about the question or topic you want ideas about. If anything comes to you when you wake up, write it down. Also, when you first wake up, ask yourself the question or state the topic you want ideas about, and write down any ideas that now come to you. Later you can pick out the best ideas in order to act on them.

8) Find an idea buddy with whom you can share ideas and brainstorm together. Take turns coming up with ideas for each other. When it is your turn to get ideas, tell your buddy where you feel stuck or what you want ideas about to help you move forward. Then, let you buddy give you suggestions. Just listen and don't try to critique any ideas. Write them down to help you remember. Then, put the ideas you like best into action. Similarly, give your buddy ideas when it is his or her to ask for your help.

9) Break whatever you are doing into smaller pieces or tasks which you can do in an hour or two. Then, create a timeline for when to do those tasks and work on those tasks during the time you set for doing them. You can always push the task ahead to a future time, but focus on doing that task in the here and now. The more you do this, the more you can come up with ideas and put them into practice.

10) If you find you are resisting doing something, take some time to ask yourself why you are doing this, when you meditate or exercise and listen to what comes to you. Then, ask yourself what you can do to overcome whatever is holding you back, or should you do something else and if so, what? Then, listen to the answer and put that response into action.

CHAPTER 9: THE 10 BIGGEST MISTAKES WRITERS MAKE IN PUBLISHING THEIR FIRST BOOK

Over 90% of self-published books sell less than 100 copies because of the mistakes writers make. Here are the things to do to avoid the biggest mistakes.

Use the blank page before each tip to write down your thoughts about how to apply that tip in your own writing, publishing, and promotion.

1) Make sure it's well written without typos, and a professional editor can help. Reviewers can be very picky and can give you a bad review because of writing mistakes.

2) Have a really good cover, because that's the first thing prospective readers see, and a good cover helps to showcase your book and show it's going to be good. A poorly designed cover screams self-publishing by an amateur, so you want to avoid that.

3) Plan to actively promote and market your book so it doesn't get lost in the millions of books that have been published. That includes doing a prelaunch, launch, and post-launch campaign.

4) In doing your prelaunch, launch, and post-launch campaign, use advertising, book promotion sites, YouTube videos, social media postings, press releases, and other methods to drum up sales for our book.

5) Get at least 5 reviews and testimonials. To do so, set a low introductory price on Kindle — .99 or $1.99, and appeal to friends, associates, members of referral and networking groups, and social media contacts to buy it there or offer to reimburse those who buy a paperback.

6) Don't limit your sales to Amazon. So don't give Amazon the rights to extended distribution or sign-up for KDP Select if you plan to reach beyond Amazon and publish on other platforms besides KDP and Kindle which Amazon owns.

    For example, these other platforms include hardcover, paperback, and e-books with IngramSpark for sales to bookstores and libraries and Draft2Digital for e-book distribution to other outlets, such as Apple Book and Barnes and Noble.

7) To get bookstore and library sales, get your ISBNs for paperback, hardcover, and ebooks through Myidentifiers.com, which is a part of Bowker. Then, using those ISBNs, publish your books through IngramSpark. When you publish on KDP, you can either get a free ISBN from Amazon or bring your own your book has its own identity, separate from Amazon.

8) To get additional e-book sales, set up your accounts for digital versions of your book through the online book aggregators, such as Smashwords or Draft2Digital, which will distribute your e-book to about 10 other retailers of online book.

9) Don't try to do everything yourself, so you can spend more time writing, speaking about your book, or doing programs based on it. Instead, get help with marketing and promotion by working with a social media expert, publicist, web site designer, virtual assistant, and others to create a support team.

10) Look for ways to tie what you are writing about to something in the news, which will help you get publicity for your book.

CHAPTER 10: 10 WAYS TO FIND AND WORK WITH A VIRTUAL ASSISTANT

In today's Internet and social media age, you have to do all kinds online promotion to increase your visibility, credibility, and authority, if you are marketing any kind of book, product, or service. Even local businesses catering to the local market usually need some online presence. Given the many marketing options, it's easy to get overwhelmed by all the online channels, strategies, and activities to keep up. That's why hiring a virtual assistant can help you manage the many activities you want to do online, because you don't have the time or ability to do it all.

Many virtual assistants work on their own; some are part of a company with a team of virtual assistants; and you can hire them in the U.S. or in many other countries where the cost is much less, such as the Phillippines, India, Sri Lanka, Pakistan, and Nigeria

What can they do for you, where do you find them, and how much can you expect to pay. The following tips will get you started. As you read each tip, write down your thoughts about what to do. Perhaps make a spreadsheet to keep track of what you do and the results. This will help you decide what methods work best.

1) Make a list of the routine everyday tasks you don't like or don't have time to do, for which you could easily get someone else to do these tasks. Also, list additional tasks you would like to do to build your business and get more clients, but don't have the time or ability to do yourself. These are the kind of tasks where a virtual assistant can help.

2) A virtual assistant can do a variety of online research, marketing, social media, and other tasks. Different assistants will offer a different range of activities. For example, some will do transcripts for about $1 a page, along with various editorial tasks, such as proofreading and editing contact. Some will do PR, creating media lists for you using Cisicion's media data base. And some will handle your scheduling, payments, invoicing, web research, and monitor and respond to emails. Depending on their experience and the work they will do, their pay will range from $20 to $75 an hour in the U.S., about $10 to $15 an hour in some other countries.

One way to keep track of who does what for what cost is to create a spreadsheet where you lists the tasks you want done on one side and the names of the virtual assistants you contact on top. Then, check off who does what and include their hourly rates or package for a certain number of hours and activities.

3) Here the kinds of research tasks a VA can do:
- Create a media list for local or national print, radio, podcast, and TV sources, such as by using the Cision media database or a list you purchase.
- Create a list of trade associations, service organizations, corporations, non-profits, or trade associations in your industry or community, which might be interested in your products or services or articles from you for their newsletter. Some might be interested in having you speak to their organization.
- Find online groups that might be interested in your products or services, such as on Facebook, LinkedIn, Twitter, and Yahoo. The VA can then post on these groups using copy you or they write.
- Find bloggers that appeal to your target audience, and then pitch them on doing a guest blog or inviting them to interview you for a story.
- Find websites of others in your field, so you can compare your website to theirs to improve your own. Or perhaps they might reach out to these website contacts to suggest ways you might do joint promotions or otherwise work together.

4) Here are some marketing tasks a VA can do:
- Create and manage an online group for you, such as on Facebook, LinkedIn, Twitter, or Yahoo.
- Set up an online promotion to create an email list, so you can contact those on this list with additional offers, newsletters, and information about new books, products, and programs. The way getting these emails works is you offer a free gift, like a product sample or report on industry news, and you create a landing page or page on your website where people can get the gift in return for putting in their email. Once they do this, an automatic responder sends the gift or access to it in an email. This way they get the gift, which may lead them to want to hire you or buy more products from you, and you have a valid email for them which you can use in email marketing.
- Do regular mailings to your email list, using a program like GetResponse, AWeber, Constant Contact, or MailChimp.
- Offer review copies of your book or product to reviewers, such as to the top reviewers on Amazon.

5) Here are some publicity tasks a VA can do:
- Keep track of any mentions of you, such as on Google Alerts, where you can get info about news, products, or mentions of your name. Just go to Google Alerts (www.google.com/alerts) to indicate what you want to be notified about. Or as an alternative, go to Talkwalker Alerts (www.talkwalker.com/alerts) which similarly brings every mention of your brand across the internet, including from websites, blogs, forums, and even Twitter to your inbox.
- Keep track of and reply to any media opportunities that are offered through the two main services that send out announcements about reporters who are looking for sources to interview. These are HARO (help a reporter out: www.helpareporter.com) and PitchRate (pitchrate.com/wphome).

6) Here are some social media tasks a VA can do:
- Do regular posts to the major social media platforms, such as Facebook, Twitter, LinkedIn, and Instagram, using a tool like HootSuite or Buffer, to schedule regular posting every day or two or several times a day.
- Keep track of your social media responses, such as comments and questions, and reply to them.
- Boost your posts or create ads for you on Facebook, Instagram, and other social media.
- Update information about you, your company, and your products and services, wherever you have bio information.
- Find photos for you from stock photo houses to use in social media posts.

7) Here are ways VAs can help with your website and blog:
- Post new blogs to your website and moderate any comments, if you allow comments, so only the favorable ones get posted.
- Send out invitations to others who write blogs for your target audience, so they can write their articles for your blog. This can result in more viewers for you, since these other bloggers will let their own followers know about their post.
- Find images to enhance your blogs, such as from stock photo services, like Shutterstock.com, Adobestock.com, iStockPhoto.com, Dreamstime.com, 123rf.com, or Pixabay.com, which is free.
- Review your website pages to look for any editorial errors. VAs can also check that the keywords for your business are sprinkled through each page on the site, which will increase your site rankings and make you more findable, when individuals search for products and services like yours.

8) You can find virtual assistants in various ways.
- Sometimes they are members of local business and networking groups.
- You can find local VAs by putting "virtual assistants" and "near me" in Google Search.
- You can find them through various platforms, such as Upwork.com, Fiverr.com, and Thumbtack.com.
- Other sources include uassistme.co, virtualemployee.com, vivavirtual.com, and zirtual.com.
- You can make a request for a VA through the International Virtual Assistants Association (ivaa.org/directory) or the Virtual Assistants Directory (virtualassistant.directory)
- Ask business associates if they can refer you to a virtual assistant they or a contact has worked with.

9) Since there are so many sources for hiring a virtual assistant, ideally get referrals and recommendations for prospective VAs. Generally, it's best to send an email to the VA to get a list of their services, packages, and costs. Then, narrow down your search to those offering the services you want and other factors you consider important, such as hourly rate, cost of a package, and the VAs location if you want someone near you.

10) Talk to the VA about what you want to first and what the VA recommends. Generally, figure on starting with 5 to 10 hours to see how well the VA will work for you.

For example, I hired one VA who had a 10 to 12 hour PR package, with a sliding scale from $75 to $55 an hour, based on how many hours I retained her for. I hired another VA to do a series of social media posts and responses for 10 hours at $20 an hour.

In other words, you might hire different VAs to do different things at different price points based on their experience. Then, monitor the results. If you like what the VA does and get a good response to any marketing, publicity, or social media posts, you can continue to work together.

Now good luck in finding and working with a virtual assistant. And besides the tasks suggested here, you may have other ideas on what you want a VA to do.

ABOUT THE AUTHOR

GINI GRAHAM SCOTT, Ph.D., J.D., is a nationally known writer, consultant, speaker, and seminar leader, specializing in business and work relationships, professional and personal development, social trends, and popular culture. She has published 50 books with major publishers. She has worked with dozens of clients on memoirs, self-help, popular business books, and film scripts. Writing samples are at www.changemakerspublishingandwriting.com.

She is the founder of Changemakers Publishing, featuring books on work, business, psychology, social trends, and self-help. The company has published over 150 print, e-books, and audiobooks. She has licensed several dozen books for foreign sales, including the UK, Russia, Korea, Spain, and Japan.

She has received national media exposure for her books, including appearances on *Good Morning America, Oprah,* and *CNN*. She has been the producer and host of a talk show series, *Changemakers*, featuring interviews on social trends.

Scott is active in a number of community and business groups, including the Lafayette, Pleasant Hill, and Walnut Creek Chambers of Commerce. She is a graduate of the prestigious Leadership Contra Costa program. She does workshops and seminars on the topics of her books.

She is also the writer and executive producer of 10 films in distribution, release, or production. Her most recent films that have been released include *Driver, The New Age of Aging,* and *Infidelity*.

She received her Ph.D. from the University of California, Berkeley, and her J.D. from the University of San Francisco Law School. She has received five MAs at Cal State University, East Bay, most recently in Communication.

OTHER AVAILABLE BOOKS ON INSPIRATION, MOTIVATION, AND SUCCESS

Control Your Life, Control Your Thoughts
Pursue Your Passion
Work It Right
The Courage Book
The Gratitude Book
The Anger Book
The Forgiveness Book
The Vision Board Book
Affirming Your Success
Animal Insights
The Animal Experience
20 Rhymes for Your Success
Turn Your Dreams into Reality
The Wisdom of Water: To Your Success
The Wisdom of Water: Insights from Nature for Everyday Life
Mind Power: Picture Your Way to Success in Business
The Empowered Mind: How to Harness the Creative Force Within

CHANGEMAKERS PUBLISHING
3527 Mt. Diablo Blvd., #273
Lafayette, CA 94549
changemakers@pacbell.net . (925) 385-0608
www.changemakerspublishingandwriting.com